Living With Grief

A Guide for Your First Year of Grieving

Brook Noel and Pamela D. Blair, Ph.D

A GRIEFSTEPS® GUIDE

www.griefsteps.com

adapted from *I Wasn't Ready to Say Goodbye*
by Brook Noel and Pamela D. Blair, Ph.D.

Also by Brook Noel & Pamela D. Blair, Ph.D.
I Wasn't Ready to Say Goodbye: surviving, coping and healing
    after the sudden death of a loved one
I Wasn't Ready to Say Goodbye Companion Workbook
Living with Grief: a guide for your first year of grieving

By Brook Noel
Back to Basics: 101 Ideas for Strengthening Our Children and
    Our Families
The Single Parent Resource
Surviving Holidays, Birthdays and Anniversaries: a guide for
    grieving during special occasions

Order online at www.championpress.com
or at www.griefsteps.com

CHAMPION PRESS, LTD.
FREDONIA, WISCONSIN
Copyright © 2003 Brook Noel

ISBN: 1891400088
Library of Congress Information Available Upon Request
Manufactured in the United States of America 10 9 8 7

From Brook Noel...

This book is for all the wonderful people who have
shared their stories with me. Your e-mails have
touched me and encouraged me. Thank you all for
taking the time to share your journey.
I look forward to "seeing" all of you at
www.griefsteps.com

Contents

Chapter One
Notes for the Start of Your
Journey...

*"What we call the beginning is often the end.
To make an end is to make a beginning.
The end is where we start from."*
T.S. Eliot

At this moment, in the direct aftermath of losing someone tragically, there is so little anyone can say. We cannot find the words to offer you peace—though we wish it a gift we could give you. We promise you now that we will give you everything we can to help you make your way through this. We will help you wind a path through the haze, the confusion and the pain that is gripping at your core.

For the first few months, do not concern yourself with what you will do, where you will go or what lies in the future. For now, we ask that you simply follow the guidelines in this chapter. There will be time to cope, to understand, to process—later. Right now, you simply need to take care of yourself.

Treat Yourself as if You Were in Intensive Care

You are in the process of going through one of the most traumatic experiences a person can endure. The challenges you have already faced both physically and mentally will leave you vulnerable, exhausted and weak. It is imperative that you focus directly on yourself and on any dependents. Find ways to get your needs met in these first few weeks.

If you have small children, contact friends and relatives to help you care for them. Consider having someone stay with you for the specific task of caring for your children since some children may be further traumatized by separation. In Chapter Nine we cover the specifics of children and grief. While it is human nature to want to help and care for others, we must understand at this trying time we will barely have enough energy to care for ourselves. Even if we want to help those around us, we won't have the resources. It's in our best interest to allow this time for our own grief.

Someone to Take Calls

If the person that has died is of your immediate family, you will be receiving many phone calls, visitors and cards. Have a friend come by to take messages, answer the door and answer the phone. Most callers do not expect to speak directly with the family but simply wish to express their condolences. Have someone keep a notepad handy to record the names and messages of callers.

Be forewarned, occasionally you may receive a strange call or a strange card. On one occasion Brook took a message from a caller that offered condolences for the loss of her brother and then in a second breath requested a current picture of her daughter. Pam remembers a caller who said, "I'm sure George's death was easier for you, because you were divorced after all." These thoughts and comments are inappropriate and can be very hurtful, though the caller does not intend them to be. In our society, we just don't know how to handle grief and loss. People cope with grief differently—many people don't know how to cope at all. When you think about it, our world is geared toward gaining and acquiring; we have few lessons on how to handle losing and loss. Occasionally people will ask a strange question or perhaps write a note in a card that seems a bit "out of place". Realize that this is not done to hurt you; these are just people who are inept at handling loss or the thought of loss.

Seek Assistance

In addition to getting help to answer the phone, seek out your most trusted friend to help with any final arrangements that are your responsibility. You may be the person who needs to organize the funeral service or you may have insurance agencies to contact or an estate to settle. While you can, and should be involved in these areas at some level, it is important to find someone who can do most of the calling for you, make trips to the funeral home, find out information and then let you make the final choices. In the direct aftermath of loss your judgment may be impaired and a trusted friend can act as a guide in decision making. In the Appendix of this book, you will find some worksheets that will guide you and your support person through these processes.

Don't Worry about Contacting People

In the first few days you will make initial calls to immediate family and friends. Beyond that, try to limit the number of calls for which you are personally responsible. At this time, you are unlikely to have the energy or the will to make these calls. If there are additional calls that need to be made, seek out the assistance of a trusted friend.

Additionally, you may want to obtain the deceased's address book and let your trusted friend contact the people within.

Let Your Body Lead You

Grief affects us all differently. Some of us may become very active and busy, while others may become lethargic or practically comatose. Let your body lead you. If you feel tired—sleep. If you feel like crying—cry. If you are hungry—eat. Don't feel you need to act one way or another. There are no "shoulds" right now, simply follow the lead of your body.

One caution: With the shock of losing someone tragically it is not uncommon for people to turn to medication. This can be as minor as a sleeping aid or as major as consuming large amounts of alcohol. Try to resist these urges. This will not make the grief easier. If you must engage in some sort of self-medication be aware that this will not take away from any of the grief you are feeling, it will simply postpone your grief until you cease the self-medication.

Religious Traditions

If you were married or your loved one adopted a religion you are unfamiliar with, you may encounter traditions that are uncomfortable for you. The religious requirements around death and burial may cause confusion and unrest in the family and among friends.

For example, Marjory comes from a family where a wake lasts for days and cremation is preferred. Since Marjory was the custodial parent, she took her son to Sunday school on a regular basis. When her young son died unexpectedly, her ex-husband, a religious Jew, was adamantly against the plans she was making. Some Jews are required to bury their dead within 24 hours and believe that cremation is a most undignified method of disposing a body. Also, after the immediate burial, Jews "sit shiva" for seven days with the nearest of kin.

It is so very important at a tragic time like this to be caring and understanding of the traditions of both the deceased and the families involved. To honor the deceased, the living must find equal ways to compromise. In Marjory's case, because most of her family had been uninvolved in her son's life and her ex-husband's family had been so close to her, she decided on burial for her son instead of cremation. Her ex-husband in turn agreed to participate in the Christian-oriented wake Marjory had planned.

If you are unclear about what is best for you, your family or your loved one, seek counsel with a clergy person, family mediator or therapist. In dual faith situations where decisions are difficult, the services of an Interfaith Minister might be helpful. You can contact the Association of Interfaith Ministers for a referral by phone at 203-855-0000 or by e-mail at: aim@interfaithclergy.org

Keep in mind that peoples' needs will be different. When Brook's brother died, they held a small informal viewing for close friends. Many of Caleb's friends chose not to attend. They preferred to remember Caleb as they had seen him last. Others found the viewing helpful. There is no right or wrong way to grieve, it's simply important to be open and respectful of individual needs.

Wills and Arrangements

While those that die a lingering death often have wills and have told the living what they would like as far as funerals, burial, etc., one who dies a sudden death has frequently not indicated to friends and family how they would like to be treated in death. This presents an extra burden for loved ones, since they are required to go ahead with arrangements under assumptions of what their loved one may have wanted. With our emotional and physical levels depleted, these decisions become even harder. You may find it helpful to discuss your options with a group of close friends that knew the deceased. When Brook and her mother were trying to figure out what type of service to hold, they talked to each other first, and then asked Caleb's friends for input and ideas. With the help of others, they decided a celebration in his honor would be the way he would choose to be remembered. Since the decision had been a group effort, everyone felt comfortable.

Expect to be Distracted

During the first few weeks your mind will be filled with racing thoughts and unfamiliar emotions. Many people report having difficulty with simple tasks.

Losing one's keys, forgetting where you are while driving and sluggish reaction time are all commonly reported problems. With everything you are mentally and physically trying to process, it's normal to be distracted. Take special caution. Try to avoid driving and other activities where these symptoms may cause injury.

Have Someone Near You

If possible, choose a close friend to keep near you through the first week or two. Let this person help you make decisions, hear your fears or concerns and be the shoulder for you to lean on. Give them a copy of this book. Later as you move through the grieving process it will be very helpful to have someone who has "been there" and thoroughly understands what you are talking about.

The Help of Friends

Our energy is so depleted in the first few weeks after loss, it's hard to even ask for help. We have included a handout on the following pages that can be photocopied freely and given to your inner circle of friends and relatives. You may be reluctant to do this, but please do. Even if we don't think we need people right now, we do indeed. The cycle of your grief will be more bearable when you hold the hand of a friend. Reach out.

These days will be long and challenging and there may seem to be no resolution for any of the pains that plague you. That's all right. It's all right to feel hopeless and as if all has lost its purpose. These are natural and normal feelings. Trust that life will go on, and that in time, you will reestablish your place within it. For now, simply take care of yourself. In a few weeks return to this book or refer to it as needed. Trust that there will be light again and know this book will be here for you in a month or so when you're ready to begin dealing and coping more intricately with your journey through grief.

A Guide for Helping Others with Grief
(photocopy and give to close
friends and loved ones)

Don't try to find the magic words or formula to eliminate the pain. Nothing can erase or minimize the painful tragedy your friend or loved one is facing. Your primary role at this time is simply to "be there." Don't worry about what to say or do, just be a presence that the person can lean on when needed.

Don't try to minimize or make the person feel better. When we care about someone, we hate to see them in pain. Often we'll say things like, "I know how you feel," or "perhaps, it was for the best," in order to minimize their hurt. While this can work in some instances, it never works with grief.

Help with responsibilities. Even though a life has stopped, our lives do not. One of the best ways to help is to run errands, prepare food, take care of the kids, do laundry and help with the simplest of maintenance.

Don't expect the person to reach out to you. Many people say, "call me if there is anything I can do." At this stage, the person who is grieving will be overwhelmed at the simple thought of picking up a phone. If you are close to this person, simply stop over and begin to help. People need this but don't think or are too depleted to ask. There are many friends that will be there during the good times— but few that are there in life's darkest hour, when we need them most.

Talk through decisions. While working through the grief process many bereaved people report difficulty with decision making. Be a sounding board for your friend or loved one and help them think through their decisions.

Don't be afraid to say the name of the deceased. Those who have lost someone usually speak of them often, and believe it or not, need to hear the deceased's name and stories. In fact, many grievers welcome this.

Remember that time does not heal all wounds. Your friend or loved one will change because of what has happened. Everyone grieves differently. Some will be "fine" and then experience their true grief a year later, while others grieve immediately. There are no timetables, no rules—be patient.

Remind the bereaved to take care of themselves. Eating, resting and self-care are all difficult tasks when besieged by the taxing emotions of grief. You can help by keeping the house stocked with healthy foods that are already prepared or (easy-to-prepare). Help with the laundry. Take over some errands so the bereaved can rest. However, do not push the bereaved to do things they may not be ready to do. Many grievers say, "I wish they would just follow my lead." While it may be upsetting to see the bereaved withdrawing from people and activities—it is normal. They will rejoin as they are ready.

Avoid judging. Don't tell the person how to react or handle their emotions or situation. Simply let him/her know that you support their decisions and will help in any way possible.

Share a Meal. Invite the bereaved over regularly to share a meal or take a meal to their home since meal times can be especially lonely. Consider inviting the bereaved out on important dates like the one-month anniversary of the death, the deceased's birthday, the grievers birthday and other significant dates.

Make a list of everything that needs to be done with the bereaved. This could include everything from bill paying to plant watering. Prioritize these by importance. Help the bereaved complete as many tasks as possible. If there are many responsibilities, find one or more additional friends to support you.

Make a personal commitment to help the one who is grieving get through this. After a death, many friendships change or disintegrate. Often people don't know how to relate to the one who is grieving, or they get tired of being around someone who is sad. Vow to see your friend or loved one through this, to be their anchor in their darkest hour.

Excerpted from "I Wasn't Ready to Say Good-bye: a guide for surviving, coping and healing after the sudden death of a loved ones" by Brook Noel and Pamela D. Blair, Ph.D. (Champion Press, 2000)

Chapter Two
Understanding the
Emotional & Physical
Affects of Grief

"When people ask me what I was feeling... I didn't know how to respond. I wasn't feeling any one emotion—I was feeling everything—all at the same time." **Anonymous**

The unexpected loss of someone close to us can quickly turn our world into an unfamiliar place. Coping with what used to be routine, becomes exhausting. The simplest task may seem daunting. Grief affects us not only emotionally, but also physically. When we are able to understand how grief affects us, we are better equipped to deal with its grip. While we wish we never had to learn or understand these emotions, being aware of them may offer us comfort in our own times of sorrow. A common feeling for people dealing with tragic loss, is the feeling of going crazy. The emotions are so strong and intense, those grieving often think they are the only ones to feel that way or that their feelings are wrong. In the pages to come, we have included many of these emotions. You're not crazy and you're not alone. By understanding these emotions, we take the first step toward realization and thus our first step on the pathway of healing.

In her book, *A Journey Through Grief: Gentle, Specific Help to Get You Through The Most Difficult Stages of Grief,* Alla Reneé Bozarth, Ph.D. writes, "While you are grieving, your emotional life may be unpredictable and unstable. You may feel that there are gaps in your remembered experience...You may alternate between depression and euphoria, between wailing rage and passive resignation...If you've experienced loss and are hurting, it's reasonable that your responses will be unreasonable."

In this chapter, we will explore many of the levels on which grief affects us. Some grievers report feeling many of these pains early on, while others report experiencing them later and still some report few of these experiences. Your relationship to the loved one will make your individual dance with grief unique.

Exhaustion
Perhaps the most commonly reported symptom of grief is utter exhaustion and confusion. In her book

Surviving Grief, Dr. Catherine M. Sanders explains, "We become so weak that we actually feel like we have the flu. Because of our lack of experience with energy depletion, this weakness frightens and perplexes us. Before the loss, it happened only when we were sick."

Little things we used to do without thinking, like mailing a letter, can easily become an all day task. Getting a gallon of milk can seem monumental. The thought of getting dressed, driving a car, getting money, paying a cashier, carrying the gallon, driving home—just these thoughts alone, can leave a griever hungry for sleep.

There are many remedies for exhaustion. People may prescribe vitamin combinations, exercise, eating well, staying busy and more. The suggestion of the psychotherapist is perhaps the most important: You are in recovery. Give yourself some time to grieve and let the emotions work through you. If you jump to stay busy now, or sidetrack part of the grieving process, it will only resurface down the road. It's all right to be exhausted and to rest. Take your time to heal. If, however, you have any suicidal thoughts, are not eating, become dehydrated or are suffering any additional serious symptoms, seek professional help immediately.

Days of Distraction

Most people function well in their daily lives. We know how to get things done, stay organized and accomplish what we set out to do. After experiencing a sudden death, it's as if we lose the most basic of skills. Those things that we once did with ease become difficult and challenging. Brook found distraction to be a major challenge for her during her first few months of grieving.

"I remember shortly after my brother's death, I needed to weigh two envelopes to take to the post office. I have a postage scale in my home office and I always use that to avoid holding up the line at our one-clerk, small-town post office. Well, that day I could not find the scale.

I walked through my office; through my living room. I even checked the kitchen, bedroom and bathroom. Nothing. Off and on throughout the day, I would repeat my search. For three hours, I scanned the house for that scale. Finally, in frustration, I threw my hands up and decided just to have the items weighed at the post office.

When I returned, I walked into my office and there on my desk was the scale. It had been sitting there the entire time, covered by nothing. It was in an area I had stared directly at for hours, yet I had not seen it. This is the type of distraction that often accompanies grief.

I noticed during these days, I didn't always feel down or sad, but when I was trying to cope with grief and didn't have an outlet, situations like this would occur. Many of these "days of distraction" occurred a couple of months after Caleb's death. They became an alarm for me. During these days, I would quit trying to do so much and instead, take a "time out," relax and work through my grief.

I had a similar challenge one day while trying to pay a bill. For an hour, I couldn't find my checkbook. When I finally found my checkbook, I had lost the bill that I wanted to pay. The cat-and-mouse search continued a few more times and before I knew it an entire day had passed while simply attempting to mail out a single payment. When at first this happened, I would push myself and try to keep going.

By the end of the day I was often near
tears from frustration."

These moments of distraction are signals from
your body that you must slow down. No matter how
small the task, it is too much for you right now. Be
careful not to overburden yourself. Lower your
expectations. Know that you will be able to function
like you once did—but it takes time—it takes
recovery.

Grief Knows No Schedule

In today's world we have grown accustomed to
scheduling so much of life. Most of us own at least
one organizer or appointment book. Yet grief is one
thing that will never fit in an appointment-square.
You may find there are times when you are in the
midst of a normal, pleasant activity and suddenly a
wash of grief comes over you. Know that this is
common and that grief can surface at any time,
without notice.

There is so little of life we control. Grief's timing
is among the uncontrollable. Expect experiences,
similar to these, frequently over the first three to six
months (their frequency is often based on how
close you were to the deceased). Over the course

of a year, they will lessen, but they may still happen, unexpectedly from time to time.

Physical Symptoms

When grief covers us with its dark wings, it is much like a serious illness. We will be emotionally and physically depleted and a variety of symptoms will follow. It is important to be aware of these symptoms, however, so we don't think we are going crazy. These symptoms will pass as we work through our grief. If you find any symptom to be overwhelming or unbearable, contact a professional. Here are some of the commonly reported symptoms:

chest pain	dizziness
sleep difficulties	dry mouth
poor appetite or overeating	crying
shakiness or trembling	numbness
shortness of breath	disorientation
listlessness	heart palpitations
migraines or headache	
exhaustion or weakness	

Feeling the Presence of the Deceased

Feeling the presence of the deceased is similar to a "phantom limb" syndrome, which is experienced after someone loses a limb. Many grievers feel like they have lost a part of themselves. Some spouses feel the deceased's presence in bed. Hearing footsteps, smelling that person's scent, hearing a voice or seeing a fleeting image of the deceased are common during the grief process. Often this occurs as we try to rationalize and understand what is happening. Is someone sending us a message? Are we being told something? Are we "losing" it?

In her book *Surviving Grief,* Dr. Catherine M. Sanders writes about the flicker phenomenon, "a perception seen at the outside edges of our visual field as a flickering shadow. Immediately, thoughts of the deceased come to mind, but when we look directly at that area, nothing is there."

These sightings or feelings may well be the deceased trying to comfort us, trying to get through somehow. When we try to rationalize and make sense of these experiences, we rob them of their magic. Just as we don't understand why these unexpected deaths occur, we must try not to overanalyze these moments—simply let them offer comfort.

The World Becomes Dreamlike

Many people who have lost someone suddenly, find that the world becomes a surreal place. It's almost as if we are floating without seeing or comprehending. Everything becomes a blur as the concept of time disappears. Days are measured by: one day after he died, two days after he died...all standard concepts fade away. Some have described it as slogging through molasses, a slow motion movie, a feeling like they are not in their body. Perhaps this is nature's way of slowing us down to heal.

Helen Fitzgerald, author of The *Mourning Handbook* writes, "During this initial period of grief you will feel a numbness and a disassociation with the world around you. People who are going through this often tell me that they feel as if they are watching a play in which they are but spectators. Others feel that what has happened is only a bad dream from which they will wake up to find everything back to normal." Know that this is partly the body coping with tragic loss. Our bodies and minds know better than to dump us back into reality after such an intense blow. Therefore we are nudged slowly, step-by-step, back into day-to-day life. Much of the world will remain out of focus, allowing us to gather our bearings one step at a time, one day at a time.

A Time to Withdraw

Many people will experience a state of numbness while moving through grief. The world may take on a dreamlike quality or seem to go on separately from them. Often experiences or people that once evoked joy and happiness now evoke nothing at all. Activities once enjoyed seem foreign or meaningless.

Some people spend a relatively short time in this numb state, as short as a few days, while others find it lingers. This is part of how our bodies help to protect us from the overwhelming emotions caused by our loved one's death. We become numb and filter through information as we are able, instead of all at once. Our feelings will come back, but it will take time.

Hand-in-hand with exhaustion, performing our day-to-day activities, even if they are ones we used to enjoy, may seem overwhelming. Most people are not able to maintain a variety of interests immediately after this shock. Do not make expectations for yourself to do everything. Instead, look at your commitments and try to minimize.

Contact event or group coordinators to let them know that you will be taking some time off, indefinitely. For example, if you are part of your child's home and school program, a softball coach or part of a regular bowling league—take a break. At this point you need only focus on working through these hard times. Minimize the expectations on yourself to avoid adding to your stress.

This advice runs contrary to what many will say. Many people will urge you to "stay involved," "take on more," "try something new," or "get back in the swing of things." Yet this advice doesn't make sense. If you don't have the energy or focus to take care of yourself, why should you be taking on additional responsibilities? Sure, they may take your mind off of your grief for a short period—but you still have to do your grieving. There simply is no bypass.

Impulsive Living

While some grievers withdraw, others will compulsively pursue activities. Their thought process often goes like this, "Life is short. I'd better do everything now that I always wanted to do... spend all the money, sell the house and move to

Hawaii, write that book, divorce my wife, etc."
Others will take unnecessary risks.

It is imperative to carefully monitor your behavior during the first year. Do not make impulsive decisions. Do not sell your house, change locations, divorce a partner., etc. Wait until the fog has lifted and you can clearly see the options available to you.

Instant Replays and Obsessive Thoughts

At some point in our grief work, we are likely to find ourselves recounting the days with our loved one in our minds. We may also play out different scenarios of the death, trying to understand what has happened. For some, the review completely preoccupies the mind, and despite our wishes we can think of nothing else.

As is the case with post traumatic stress disorder, you may find yourself living and reliving the experiences you had with your loved one during the days, hours or minutes just before the death occurred. "If only I had not taken that road...If only I had said 'don't go...' If only I had been there I might have prevented the accident..." and on and on.

With the first news of loss, our mind acts as a filter. It immediately sifts through the facts and details offering only the barest to keep us informed. Too much detail would be more than we could bear. So our mind filters and filters until our bodies and hearts can cope with a little more. At some point, when the body has recovered somewhat, the mind lets larger blocks of information in. At this point, by human instinct, we look for resolution. We struggle to make sense of what has happened and that is where the instant replay begins. We explore every option—even the outlandish. These explorations are what allow us to slowly internalize the fact that life, as we once knew it, has changed.

This is a pivotal point in the grieving process. At this point, or close to it, we are finally acknowledging the death in reality, with the "if only" mind game

"If only" is the game of guilt that plagues many survivors. The "if only" questions surface intensely in cases of unexpected death. The situation is so "out of control" that our human nature fights and searches for a way to control the uncontrollable. As we yearn to make sense of the senseless, often the only route of control we find is to blame ourselves.

"I should have known," or "If only I had talked to him for two minutes longer..." are sentiments that those who grieve may say to themselves over and over. Realize this guilt is a way of trying to gain control over the uncontrollable, and then, work to let it go. Each time it enters, remember that this is our longing for control, but don't give in to the guilt. You cannot change what has happened and odds are you couldn't have changed it beforehand. No one knows these things are going to happen—no one has that much control. Brook found that she ran on the "I should've known" treadmill.

"I have talked with many of the people surviving the loss of a loved one and in every situation the one who is grieving can somehow tie blame to themselves. Even with my brother's case, where it was such a freak accident, we could all find ways that we "should have known" or "should have been able to prevent it." Yet as each of us told our stories of prevention, others could see there were simply too many holes. None of us could have stopped what occurred."

Don't run yourself around this wheel of pain. If you find that you cannot stop trying to tie the blame to yourself, relay your story to a professional counselor, therapist or pastor. While we grieve, we are not objective. These professionals can help us to see how unrealistic and unfounded our thoughts can be.

Anger

Who wouldn't be angry when someone they loved so dearly is suddenly taken from them? Anger is natural in this situation and is actually a healthy part of the grieving process. Yet anger takes different forms, some of them healthy and some of them unhealthy.

Let's examine the types of anger that are natural, though unhealthy. Some of us will express anger when we are not getting the support we need from friends, family or work. While intensely wrapped in our grief, we usually don't think to ask for support. Instead we lash out at those close to us with hostility, irritability and anger. If we can recognize this anger for what it is, we can use it in a healthy way. This can be our cue that we are not receiving the support that we need. We need to ask for more or seek out other support networks.

Displaced anger is simply misdirected anger. We want someone to take responsibility for what has happened. We need someone to blame and to be held accountable. We may scream or yell at those who cared for the person at the hospital. We may become angry with those who were with the person when he died. Displaced anger is completely natural and will lessen as you learn to accept what has happened.

Anger can also surface when we recall past moments or turmoil, pain or unresolved anger within our relationship with the person we have lost. Suddenly we are forced to realize we will never share another physical interaction with this person. When that happens, memories flood through. Within these memories there are bound to be recollections of feisty exchanges, arguments and past hurts. Wishing we had more time with the loved one, we may over-criticize ourselves for any time there was conflict in the past. It is unrealistic, however, to expect perfection in any relationship. Immersing ourselves in the "should haves" and "could haves" of the past will only prevent us from dealing effectively with anger in the present.

Anger also occurs when we suppress our feelings. Anger is not the most accepted emotion in today's culture. In fact, many people don't even recognize anger as part of the grieving process. Depending on our support network and situation we may be encouraged not to show our anger. When this happens, our anger still exists and needs to be released, so it is released inward. This can cause a variety of problems. We may become sick, depressed, have chronic pain or begin having nightmares. Begin to look at healthy alternatives for releasing this anger.

Anger is especially common with tragic deaths. Since we could do nothing to stop or prevent the loss, and are left only to interpret it, we may become frustrated and develop feelings of helplessness. Bouts of crying are the most common release for this anger. It's easy to not release this anger and to turn it inward. If you suspect you may be doing so, talk to a friend or counselor to help release these feelings.

Appropriate anger is a point that we all hope to get to eventually. In this phase we can take our anger, in whatever form, and vent it. There are many ways to release anger appropriately. Here are a few...

- beat a pillow
- create a sacred space where you can go and not be heard or seen to let the anger out of your system

- use journaling to record and release your angry feelings
- take a walk out into an unpopulated area and scream until you are exhausted
- talk with a friend, therapist or counselor
- see the appendix for other ideas

Fear

Throughout our grief work, fear can be debilitating. Some people experience fear in a small number of areas, while others are overwhelmed by it. It is perfectly natural to be fearful. We have experienced the most unexpected tragedy. Common fears include: fearing any situation that remotely resembles how the loved one died, fearing that others we love will be harmed, fearing we will be unable to go on, fearing we will die ourselves and fearing the simplest activities will lead to tragedy.

Fear serves several purposes. In the initial stages of grief it gives us something to focus on besides the death that has taken place. It also offers potential control. If we fear that riding in a car could kill us, and choose not to ride in a car, we create the illusion of control. As explained earlier, with tragic death it's common to seek any control we can find. Most of the time, fear will run its course naturally. If you find that you have any fear that is, or is becoming, debilitating, talk to a professional.

As you think about this chapter, remember that grief will be a unique experience for each one of us. If you experience symptoms that are not listed here, or less symptoms than listed, that is okay and normal. What is important to remember, is that you need to work through the feelings you do feel. Sometimes we will require another person's help. Monitor yourself on your path through grief. You know, in your heart of hearts, whether you are walking down the path, or stuck at the beginning, or mired in the middle. There are many things we must face in life alone, grief need not be one of them when we reach out to one another.

Chapter Three
Grief and Dreams

"Shock has rearranged our insides. The disorientation comes from not yet recognizing the new arrangement. Grief is a molting where we shed the parts of us that are no longer applicable to the new parts. It isn't a time to understand anything."
Stephanie Ericsson,
Companion Through Darkness

Some people have dreams of the deceased and others do not. Each of our subconscious minds copes with life differently. You probably know people who remember their dreams and others who rarely remember a thing. Similarly, how grief affects us in our dream-world varies. If you don't have dreams of the deceased, don't worry.

If You Don't Dream

In *Intuition* magazine, Marlene King wrote an article entitled, "The Surrogate Dreamers: One couple's gift to a grieving friend." Marlene invited a couple she knew over for a causal Saturday night barbecue. The next night, Stephen, the 44-year-old husband of the couple died of heart failure while dancing with his wife. Over the next week Marlene helped her friend with details surrounding the tragic death. Marlene writes, "It was during this period that Janice told me she hoped to connect with Stephen through her dreams, but no dreams had come. Knowing that emotions often block us physically, I reassured her that her dreams would return, when she was less emotionally fragile."

A few days after this conversation, Marlene dreamt of Stephen. She saw him dressed in a tuxedo. She felt this odd, since Stephen usually dressed casually. She goes on to say, "I reported the dream to Janice...the absolute silence and lack of response on the other end of the phone made me question whether I was right to tell her about the dream. Unknown to me, she had elected to have Stephen cremated the day before, and had chosen to dress him in the same clothing he wore in my dream. For a while after that, it was as though both my husband and I became Janice's 'surrogate dreamers.' Our love for her seemed to open us up to the dream communication that was temporarily unavailable to Janice due to her shattered emotional state."

If you find that you are not having dreams, know that this is normal. Our emotions can be so turbulent during these times that we are cut off from our dream source. Listen to others close to you. Listen to family and friends. What dreams are they having? If they don't bring it up, ask if you like. Their dreams can carry messages for you as well.

If You Do Dream
A Dream Journal

Consider keeping a dream journal. Many people believe that dreams following closely after death are the deceased making contact. These dreams may be ones that you want to cherish and hold. If you remember your dreams, spend ten minutes each morning jotting down thoughts and impressions in your dream journal. If you only remember pieces of your dream, jot those down. Often just a few notes will spur other recollections.

Dreams of your deceased loved one can open up new avenues to healing, but you may not be aware you are having dreams or they may be hard to remember. One way to keep the dream upon waking is to keep still—don't move a muscle—don't get up to go to the bathroom or turn on the light. Start with any dream fragment that comes to your conscious mind and try to piece the entire dream back together. Or, simply write down the dream fragment and the rest may come back later in the day. In her book, Nature's Prozac, Judith Sachs offers the following thoughts on remembering dreams, "Before you go to sleep at night, put a pad and pen on your bedside table. Tell yourself you are going to remember your dreams (this suggestion may take a few nights to penetrate.) As you relax in bed, give yourself permission to explore all the areas of your mind that you don't pay enough attention to during the day. We tend to be in REM sleep just before waking, so it's best to set your radio alarm to a soft music station rather than to the news or hard rock. This way you can wake slowly and take stock of what's going on in your mind."

Troublesome Dreams

Some grievers report nightmares or troublesome dreams. These dreams may involve a direct conflict between the dreamer and the deceased. Other times the dreamer may envision the deceased dying or in pain.

With sudden death we often have very little information. Dreams are where our subconscious mind works things through. If you awake from an unpleasant dream, realize it is your subconscious mind prompting you. Recall as much as you can. Try to fill in the blanks. Examine the dream the best you can. If you find it hard to face these dreams or have problems being objective, ask a trusted friend or psychotherapist to review them with you. Keeping a dream journal can also help you to make sense of troublesome dreams.

Another way to handle disturbing dreams is to try to "re-program" them. Think through your upsetting dream. Try to find the point within the dream where things become upsetting. Choose a different ending that would make you more comfortable. Visualize the dream playing out the new way in your mind several times, especially before going to sleep. This can help change or diminish the dream's impact.

If nightmares are a problem, over-the-counter or prescription medications could be the cause. According to medical researcher, Judith Sachs, if you are taking sleeping medications such as barbiturates or benzodiazepines (for anti-anxiety) these can give you nightmares. Additionally, some people have reported anti-depressants as causing vivid and shocking dreams.

Chapter Four
The World is Upside Down

"The doorbell rang at around eight-thirty. I wasn't expecting anyone, so a strange feeling came over my heart. I peeked out the keyhole, and saw my brother, Denver, and sister-in-law, Allison, standing in the hallway. I let them in. There was a deep silence, and I knew from my brother's eyes what had happened. He didn't even have to speak. He took me in his arms, and my world changed forever. My eyes moved to a picture of my son as a child, his red hair cropped close to his head, and his big blue eyes looking out at me. My world was turning to darkness, and I would never live in it the same again." **Singer Judy Collins on the death of her son, Clark.**

"I can remember staring at the sun that day and watching it fade behind the trees. I remember wishing with everything in me that the sun wouldn't go down. I knew this was the end of the last day where I had known my son alive," said one mother. As the sun sets on our days without our loved one, the world takes on a new perspective and we are forced to question our place within it.

Many grievers report feelings of everything seeming "upside down" or "wrong." In a matter of seconds, we learned that the world has changed and will never again be the same. A stage of shock follows. Unlike a terminal death where people may prepare affairs and make arrangements in advance, those facing sudden death are forced to deal with all of these things immediately. Questions and loss of purpose follow as we are forced to interpret and understand death at a time when we are not remotely prepared to do so. Spiritual questions and reassessment of one's religious faith may also occur. In this chapter we will look at the ways in which our world is turned upside down and some ideas on how to cope during this confusing time.

Assumptions are Shattered

When we grapple with sudden loss, we are forced to reconsider some assumptions about ourselves. We may begin to feel vulnerable and to experience a sense that life is tenuous. We may begin to question whether or not the world is meaningful and orderly. We may see ourselves as weak and needy for the first time. Those who haven't had to deal with the trauma of sudden death may also come to question these assumptions, but they are not forced to question the basic truth of these assumptions in the same way a sudden death survivor must.

We are all forced to confront our mortality. Most people deal with this issue in mid-life. It is then that we begin to see signs of our own aging or we face the imminent death of our parents or grandparents. This is the natural order of things. However, as survivors of sudden death we are forced to confront our own mortality at the time of the trauma— regardless of our age. A heightened sense of the fundamental fragility of life quickly emerges— usually within minutes, hours or days of the death.

Aphrodite Matsakis, Ph.D. says in her book, *Trust After Trauma,* "...although it can empower them to try to make the most out of life, it can also be frightening and overwhelming not only to themselves, but also to others who, quite understandably, prefer to avoid confronting the inevitability of their own deaths."

You may have thought, "It can't happen to me." But it did happen to someone you loved and you may no longer feel the world is a safe place. Feelings of vulnerability can bring on a sense of doom or an expectation that your own future may be foreshortened. You may experience an intense fear that the trauma may repeat itself and another family member, lover or friend will die.

Dr. Matsakis goes on to say, "The just world philosophy cannot explain what happened to you. You used to think that if you were careful, honest, and good, you could avoid disaster. But the trauma taught you that all your best efforts could not prevent the worst from happening. Perhaps you saw others who were also innocent die or be unfairly injured. So, while you would like to believe that the world is orderly, and that good is rewarded and evil is punished, you had an experience that contradicts these beliefs."

When our foundation is swept from beneath us, we begin questioning the fundamentals of life. As crazy as it seems, this shattering of assumptions is necessary in grief. We must re-evaluate what we once held as true, move through the ruin and create a new foundation based on what we have learned.

When Faith is Shattered

If our spiritual faith has been shattered, perhaps all we can expect from the grieving process is some form of transcendence. Gail Sheehy describes this beautifully in her seminal work entitled, *Pathfinders*, where she writes, "Transcendence is a realm beyond all the negative emotions of mourning, beyond even the neutral point of acceptance. When it happens that a life accident creates a pathfinder, the person is able to transcend his former self as well. A positive self-fulfilling prophecy is made as one comes out of the dark hours. And around a new work, idea, purpose, faith, or a love inspired by the accident, one's goals are realigned. Transcendence is an act of creativity. One creates a partial replacement for what has been lost. The light at the end of mourning is glimpsed, and it is cause for new joy."

It is common to question God in these dark times. We may lose faith in God, a faith we thought would never change or waiver. In *The Grief Recovery Handbook*, John W. James and Russell Freidman write, "We have to be allowed to tell someone that we're angry at God and not be judged for it, or told that we're bad because of it. If not, this anger may persist forever and block spiritual growth. We've known people who never returned to their religion because they weren't allowed to express their true feelings. If this happens, the griever is cut off from one of the most powerful sources of support he or she might have."

For most of us, this loss of faith is temporary and if we ask our clergy person or faith community, they should willingly help us with this struggle. It is common for grievers to yell, scream at God or lose faith. One should not feel guilty for such emotions. Like many other aspects of grief, this is part of our need as we work through the process.

The following anonymous poem can be comforting to recite when we are feeling lost and our faith is being tried.

Prayer of Faith

We trust that beyond absence
There is a presence.

That beyond the pain
there can be healing.

That beyond the brokenness
there can be wholeness.

That beyond the anger
there may be peace.

That beyond the hurting
there may be forgiveness.

That beyond the silence
there may be the Word.

That beyond the Word
there may be understanding.

That through understanding
there is love.

- author unknown

Redefining Ourselves

When we lose someone, we often lose a piece of
ourselves. The closer our relationship with the
person, the more of our self we have to redefine.
Much of our identity comes from our relationship to
others. Take the woman who has called herself a
wife and mother for 30 years and then loses her
family in a plane crash. This woman whose identity
was wife and mother, is left without a husband or
children. Defining ourselves by others can bring
fullness to our lives, but when faced with loss it also
means we must redefine the resulting emptiness.

One of the first things to remember as you seek
your own redefinition is that you don't need to know

all the answers now. No one will force you or hold "a clock to your head" asking you to redefine yourself over night. This is a process. It involves soul-searching, courage and rediscovery. It takes time. Realize that you don't have to let go of who you were—you just need to adapt for the future. In the case above, the mentioned woman will always know what it was like to be a wife and a mother. For the rest of her life, she will act as a wife and mother in her thoughts and actions because that is what she was for 30 years. Even though life turns itself upside down and our role may change suddenly, we can't deny the way we have lived in the past.

Simply stated, the question becomes, "Now what?" After expecting life to take a certain course, it has chosen its own, far from your plans. Again, take it slow. Choose one thing that you know for certain. If you have always loved to paint, know that in the future you can still be a painter. Focus on what you do know about yourself. Look at the things you've always wanted to try and pick one to focus on. Take it one step at a time, and as you're ready, add another "piece" to the puzzle of yourself.

What Matters?

Earlier in this chapter, we looked at the question of purpose and the paradox of how all that matters is the very present, the here and now. With that being the case, we must then turn to our priorities, goals and dreams in order to find a way to live a content lifestyle.

Many people wonder "What's life for anyway?" after losing someone tragically. All the dreams and goals we make for tomorrow seem pointless if we focus on the fact that they can be torn away without notice. "Why live for tomorrow, when it may not exist?" asked one man. In some form or another, many of us can relate to his question.

Each of us is forced to venture down our own soul path and do our own exploring. We must re-evaluate our priorities. If spending time with our family is important, then we should start now. We shouldn't work so hard in hopes of that "better day" when family can be our only focus. Instead, we must learn to incorporate our priorities, needs and dreams into a balance for our daily lives.

What are your priorities? What matters? How could you live differently? Most importantly, how could you make every day count? In many ways, the best tribute we can give to the deceased is to allow them the memorial impact of permanently changing our lives. Allow your life to fluctuate in form. Allow your priorities and loves to surface—and then live by them. When we do this, we are offering the greatest tribute to the one we have lost. In this way, we are showing them that though they have gone, they have changed our life and have influenced us to live more fully. Think about that. If you were to die tomorrow, could you think of any better legacy to leave behind than the power of helping others to live more complete lives?

Finding A Beginning, Middle and End

Questions abound, when we lose someone tragically. Unlike those who lose someone through a terminal illness, we have little or no time to question doctors, understand a diagnosis, struggle with our faith or say our goodbyes.

Yet through our upbringing we learn to understand life in terms of cycles. We understand the cycle of age. We know the cycle of schooling. We know the cycle of work. We know the cycles of diet and exercise. Almost everything can be understood as a cycle with a beginning, middle and end. Our minds will immediately try to do the same with our tragic loss experience. Our mind will look for the beginning (What happened?), the middle

(How did he/she feel, respond, progress?), the end (Was he in pain? Did he have any last thoughts or words?). Yet unless we were present, we are left with question after question. In order to get to a place where we can think about the experience in its entirety, we must know as much of the cycle as possible.

This is why it is so natural to talk with others about our loved one's last moments. Over and over again, grievers tell their stories, attempting to make sense of them, attempting to understand the cycle. Often, there are ways to get more information. Police, witnesses and doctors can all offer clues to what happened. When we have enough clues we can piece together a story that will allow our questioning to subside. As our questions lessen, we create more room to heal.

Dr. Ann Kaiser Stearns, author of *Coming Back: Rebuilding Lives After Crisis and Loss* offers the following suggestion: "Make a conscious effort to identify what is not making sense to you about your loss or crisis. You might ask yourself: What is it about the situation and/or about his or her death that is most puzzling or troubling to me? What part of grief is troubling me? What other things are troubling me?"

Before seeking your own beginning, middle and end, the following can be a useful exercise. Confront your questions. Explore your feelings and record your thoughts. Use your findings as a guideline to gather the information you will need to express a beginning, middle and end.

Why Did this Happen?

Every griever is bound to question fate and the heavens, wondering: *Why did this have to happen?* There are, of course, no concrete answers. We can speculate. We can try to create reasons to offer comfort for ourselves and our family—but in the end, we just don't know. Perhaps this is one of the hardest parts about losing someone. In our Western world we are so accustomed to having the answers. We know $2 + 2 = 4$. We know that we can send a spacecraft to the moon and back. We know that our 401K possesses X value or that our gardens will certainly begin to bloom in May. We are a culture that seeks answers and rarely rests without them.

Yet here, we face the challenge of accepting that there is no answer, at this point in time. To leave it be "only questions" is one of the most challenging demands of grief work. As poet Rainer

Marie Rilke eloquently states, "Live the questions now. Perhaps you will then gradually, without noticing it, live along some distant day into the answer."

Brook eventually garnered the trust that someday she would understand.

"Many have asked me where that trust was birthed. It came from many nights of trying to figure it out. I mapped out every possibility, every sequence of why this might have happened. None of them brought answers. In fact, few of them brought comfort. Eventually, I realized I was getting nowhere. The only way to get somewhere was to surrender to the fact that I did not know the answers. It is hard to surrender, to quit seeking, to accept the unknown.

One night I simply laid my heart at the foot of the universe. I said to the earth, to the world, 'I do not understand this and I am ready to quit trying to understand. I am ready to accept that the universe knows more than I, and that I will understand as I am ready. Until then, I ask that I am granted peace.'

Peace didn't come overnight, but it did come. And with it came a renewed faith. But it was a different faith than what I had once known. It is a faith that someone is standing by me or over me and will lead me to what I must know as I must know it. It is a faith where I surrender the unknown without expectation. I trust the process and that all will unfold in its own time."

*a caring community
for those living with loss*

Grief Steps.Com Offering 24/7 Support

Grief Steps is a program created by best-selling author Brook Noel, to reach out and provide support to the many people experiencing loss in their lives. Noel created www.griefsteps.com to offer 24/7, free internet support to anyone needing assistance during loss.

Joining is Free and Simple

Simply log onto www.griefsteps.com You will find support chats, support e-mail groups, a reading room, a free newsletter and other support services. Membership is free and the support is there for you—as little or as much as you need.

Take a step toward healing with interactive, online courses led by best-selling author Brook Noel

How do the classes work?

Its easy to get started with a GriefSteps class. Simply enroll in the course of your choice at www.griefsteps.com We offer a wide variety of classes ranging in price from $19 to $129.

What do I get with my class?

1. Once you enroll, you'll receive a welcome packet that will contain directions for the course.

2. Each class has "assignments" that you can turn in for comments from Brook Noel.

3. Each class also has a message board where you can post questions and talk to other students.

4. Each class includes a designated weekly, one-hour "chat" time. You can log on to the private chat to talk about your experiences and assignments. These chats are moderated by Brook Noel.

*Participation in chats, message boards and assignments is optional.

Healing Exercises – Part One

In this interactive, online course, you'll complete 10 different exercises that help you move forward through grief and resolve open issues. These exercises can be completed again and again after the class to further your healing. Brook Noel will comment on work you choose to turn in and encourage you in your journey.

Class length – 6 weeks   Cost $49

Now What? Living After Loss

This class offers a solid foundation for anyone wondering how to go on after loss. You'll learn what to expect physically and emotionally and how to take your first steps toward healing.

Class length – 3 weeks   Cost $19

Rituals to Honor Your Loved One

Rituals are a wonderful way to keep the memory of your loved one with you. This class will introduce you to different types of rituals and guide you in creating one of your own.

Class length – 4 weeks   Cost $29

When Will the Pain End?
Working through Unresolved Grief

Throughout this 10 week course, you'll learn about the different stages of grief and how to recognize which of your life losses have not been grieved completely. You'll learn exercises and tactics to heal and work through unresolved grief issues, which are the most common causes of sadness and depression. This is the perfect class for anyone who is having difficulty moving forward after a life loss.

Class length – 10 weeks   Cost $99

The Healing Journey: Writing through Grief

In this writing-intensive class, you'll learn how to write the story of your loss and discover its meaning. You'll create a record of your cherished memories and discover how your loved one is still in your life today. When you complete this class you will have a very special chronicle of your relationship with your loved one.

Class length – 12 weeks   Cost $129

How to Create Your Own Support Group

In this class you will be given assignments that will lead to the creation of your own support group by the completion of the course. You'll decide what type of support group you want to start (online or in-person), create materials to help spread the word and learn how to successfully guide your support group meetings.

Class length – 8 weeks   Cost $79

Basic Strategies and Exercises for Healing

In this interactive, online course, you'll complete 4 different exercises that can help you on your grief journey. You will also learn what to expect on your journey and strategies for coping.

Class length – 3 weeks   Cost $19

**Take a step toward healing.
Enroll today at <u>www.griefsteps.com</u>**

OTHER BOOKS TO HELP YOU ON YOUR JOURNEY...

Grief Steps:
10 Steps to Regroup,
Rebuild and Renew
After Any Life Loss

by Brook Noel

ISBN 1-891400-35-5
224 pages $14.95

Facing the
Ultimate Loss:
Coping with the death of
a child

By Robert J. Marx &
Susan Davidson

Hardcover 1-891400- 93-2
$23.95
Softcover 1-891400-99-1
$14.95

I Wasn't Ready to Say Goodbye:

Surviving, coping and healing after the sudden death of a loved one

by Brook Noel and Pamela D. Blair, Ph.D.

ISBN 1-891400-27-4
$14.95

also available ...
I Wasn't Ready to Say Goodbye...a companion workbook

ISBN 1-891400-50-9
$18.95

To learn more visit

www.griefsteps.com

Additional books in the GriefGuides Series
Watch for these additional titles being released in 2004. Visit www.griefsteps.com for more information or to place your order

Grief Guides are short, concise guides to assist those who are grieving specific areas in their grief journey. Each GriefGuide is $8.95 US

Surviving Grief: A Compassionate Guide for Your First Year of Grieving

Coping With the Loss of a Partner

Coping With the Loss of a Child

How to Help Someone Who Is Grieving

Surviving Holidays, Birthdays and Anniversaries: Strategies for Coping During Difficult Days

Coping with the Loss of a Sibling

Coping with the Loss of a Parent

Resource and Support for Those Who Are Grieving

Grief Exercises that Help Ease the Pain

Helping Children Cope with Grief

To order any of the products on pages 57-61 by mail, send a check or money order to Champion Press, 4308 Blueberry Road, Fredonia WI 53021. Please include $3.95 shipping and handling for any books ordered and $1 for each additional book. No shipping or handling is necessary for the online classes. Use your visa or mastercard to order online at www.griefsteps.com